IN CASE OF LOSS,
PLEASE RETURN
THIS JOURNAL TO:

....

....

....

....

....

ISBN: 978-1-7371973-0-0

First Edition. Printed in the United States of America Publisher:
Pamela J. Green Solutions, LLC, Washington DC
Editor: Susan Black

A WORD FROM YOUR EXECUTIVE COACH

Advancing to the C-Suite is not a destination; it is a journey. You stop at the side of the road for gas or to recharge your vehicle, you get something to eat, and you stay overnight to rest and recuperate. But the journey doesn't truly end until perhaps retirement, and then I wonder if you just slow down instead?

This journal is for leaders - leaders who desire to keep account of various business experiences and to capture their thoughts and ideas as a reminder not only of their goals but also of why they started down the path of leadership. What is unique about this journal is that we've added tips and tools that you can leverage to position yourself as a thoughtful and intentional leader. If you want to stay on your toes and be seen as a credible leader, you'll keep this journal nearby.

By framing your experience as a journey and not a destination, you'll likely be more willing to take note of and enjoy the scenery, gather some souvenirs, have challenging experiences, and meet some really cool people along the way. But most importantly, you never stop advancing because your focus is broader than obtaining a particular "seat"; instead, your focus is on adding value. Only those who maintain a posture of continual process improvement will retain their value.

Finally, a word of encouragement. When you hit that occasional bump in the road, and you most certainly will, do yourself a kindness and remember why you started!

Here's to the experience of a lifetime.

Pamela

IMPORTANT REMINDERS

★

Other people are attached to your success; treat them with respect.

★

You may have to shed some things in order to gain the freedom and flexibility to innovate and create in other areas.

★

You get less direction as you move up, so take the initiative for your learning.

★

Your words carry greater weight as you move up.

★

Insert yourself early into conversations.

★

Establish a rhythm for regularly meeting with your peers.

★

Understand the economics of the business - meet with the CFO to get clear on this if needed.

★

Create multiple circles: circle of trust, circle of cheerleaders and supporters, circle of collaborators, and a circle of advisors.

GOALS

Understand how decisions are made at this level.

Get clear on the financial status and how to read, interpret, and communicate it.

Know the vision, mission, and strategic direction. Connect them to your personal "why?"

Clearly articulate the strategic direction and performance of the organization.

Regularly connect with peers and senior leaders. End conversations with, "how can I help you?"

Expose your brand further by networking internally in useful and meaningful ways. Ask for introductions to key decision-makers.

Ask about and get clear on your own blind spots. Bring them into clarity for your development.

Establish a personal and professional development plan.

Get in the habit of conducting after-action reviews as part of your knowledge management process following an event, project or situation to ascertain what happened and why with a focus on how it can be done better in the future.

POWERFUL QUESTIONS

What works?

Who else needs to be in the room?

What changes in people skills and behaviors do you think will need to take place?

What is the capacity of our current talent?

What buy, borrow, or build strategies will we apply to acquire the talent needed to achieve our outcomes?

What are the facts?

What do we need to stop doing to focus on this?

What's the big picture here?

What are our choices?

What's useful about this?

What can we learn?

What is the other person thinking, feeling, needing and wanting?

What's possible here?

How does this fit into our service mix, or does it not?

To what extent does the innovation align with our other core competencies?

How can we earn or re-earn everyone's active commitment?

In what ways does this innovation disrupt current activities?

How well does the innovation support the fulfillment of our purpose?

How much risk is associated with this idea? Suggestions to mitigate the risk?

What type of communication strategy shall we adopt for this?

ONE FINAL CHECK

- [ ] I feel prepared to walk into every meeting.
- [ ] I plan for and take regular breaks throughout each day.
- [ ] I don't allow the unpreparedness of others to become my emergency.
- [ ] I have accountability partners and processes to ensure that I keep my commitments.
- [ ] I know my triggers and am improving my control and management of them.
- [ ] I routinely read books and articles to enhance my development.
- [ ] I speak up in meetings in credible and thoughtful ways.
- [ ] The pace, tone, timbre and cadence of my voice are inviting.
- [ ] I am aware of and manage my facial expressions and body language for proper effect.
- [ ] I intentionally network within the organization and outside of the organization.
- [ ] I remember the value of my contribution when under the microscope or when being scrutinized.
- [ ] My performance is top-notch.
- [ ] I lead inclusively.
- [ ] I encourage and welcome constructive feedback.
- [ ] I speak the truth in love.
- [ ] I practice emotional awareness and control and am not easily moved by external circumstances.
- [ ] I create as much distance as possible between Situations that occur and the need for a Response from me. This allows me to think through the Outcome I desire most. [S+R=O]

WORD SEARCH SOUVENIRS:

Words to boost my vocabulary

WORD SEARCH SOUVENIRS:

Words to boost my vocabulary

NOTES

Topic:	Date: / /

ACTIONS TO TAKE

Date: /   /

1
....

2
....

3
....

4
....

5
....

6
....

7
....

8
....

9
....

10
....

11
....

12
....

....

NOTES

ACTIONS TO TAKE

Date: /   /

1 ....

2 ....

3 ....

4 ....

5 ....

6 ....

7 ....

8 ....

9 ....

10 ....

11 ....

12 ....

....

NOTES

Topic:	Date: / /

....

....

....

....

....

....

....

....

....

....

....

....

....

....

....

....

....

....

....

....

....

....

ACTIONS TO TAKE

Date: /   /

1

2

3

4

5

6

7

8

9

10

11

12

NOTES

Topic:	Date: / /

ACTIONS TO TAKE

Date: /   /

1 ....

2 ....

3 ....

4 ....

5 ....

6 ....

7 ....

8 ....

9 ....

10 ....

11 ....

12 ....

NOTES

Topic:	Date: / /

ACTIONS TO TAKE

Date: / /

1

2

3

4

5

6

7

8

9

10

11

12

NOTES

Date: / /

ACTIONS TO TAKE

Date: /   /

1

2

3

4

5

6

7

8

9

10

11

12

NOTES

Topic:	Date: / /

ACTIONS TO TAKE

Date: /   /

1

2

3

4

5

6

7

8

9

10

11

12

NOTES

ACTIONS TO TAKE

Date: / /

1
....

2
....

3
....

4
....

5
....

6
....

7
....

8
....

9
....

10
....

11
....

12
....

....

NOTES

Topic:	Date: / /

ACTIONS TO TAKE

Date: / /

1

2

3

4

5

6

7

8

9

10

11

12

NOTES

Topic:	Date: / /

ACTIONS TO TAKE

Date: /   /

1
....

2
....

3
....

4
....

5
....

6
....

7
....

8
....

9
....

10
....

11
....

12
....

NOTES

Topic:	Date: / /

ACTIONS TO TAKE

Date: /   /

1
....

2
....

3
....

4
....

5
....

6
....

7
....

8
....

9
....

10
....

11
....

12
....

....

NOTES

Topic:	Date: / /

ACTIONS TO TAKE

Date: / /

1

2

3

4

5

6

7

8

9

10

11

12

NOTES

Topic:	Date: / /

ACTIONS TO TAKE

Date: /   /

1
....

2
....

3
....

4
....

5
....

6
....

7
....

8
....

9
....

10
....

11
....

12
....
....

NOTES

Topic:	Date: / /

ACTIONS TO TAKE

Date: /   /

1 ....

2 ....

3 ....

4 ....

5 ....

6 ....

7 ....

8 ....

9 ....

10 ....

11 ....

12 ....

NOTES

Topic:	Date: / /

ACTIONS TO TAKE

Date: /   /

1

2

3

4

5

6

7

8

9

10

11

12

NOTES

Topic:	Date: / /

ACTIONS TO TAKE

Date: / /

1

2

3

4

5

6

7

8

9

10

11

12

NOTES

ACTIONS TO TAKE

Date: / /

1

2

3

4

5

6

7

8

9

10

11

12

NOTES

Topic:	Date: / /

ACTIONS TO TAKE

Date: / /

1

2

3

4

5

6

7

8

9

10

11

12

NOTES

Topic:	Date: / /

ACTIONS TO TAKE

Date: /   /

1
....

2
....

3
....

4
....

5
....

6
....

7
....

8
....

9
....

10
....

11
....

12
....

NOTES

Date: / /

ACTIONS TO TAKE

1

2

3

4

5

6

7

8

9

10

11

12

NOTES

Topic:	Date: / /

ACTIONS TO TAKE

Date: / /

1

2

3

4

5

6

7

8

9

10

11

12

NOTES

ACTIONS TO TAKE

1
....

2
....

3
....

4
....

5
....

6
....

7
....

8
....

9
....

10
....

11
....

12
....

NOTES

Date: /   /

ACTIONS TO TAKE

Date: /   /

1
....

2
....

3
....

4
....

5
....

6
....

7
....

8
....

9
....

10
....

11
....

12
....

NOTES

ACTIONS TO TAKE

Date: /   /

1

2

3

4

5

6

7

8

9

10

11

12

NOTES

Topic:	Date: / /

ACTIONS TO TAKE

Date: / /

1
....

2
....

3
....

4
....

5
....

6
....

7
....

8
....

9
....

10
....

11
....

12
....

....

NOTES

Date: / /

ACTIONS TO TAKE

Date: /   /

1 ....

2 ....

3 ....

4 ....

5 ....

6 ....

7 ....

8 ....

9 ....

10 ....

11 ....

12 ....

....

NOTES

Topic:	Date: / /

ACTIONS TO TAKE

Date: /   /

1 ....

2 ....

3 ....

4 ....

5 ....

6 ....

7 ....

8 ....

9 ....

10 ....

11 ....

12 ....

....

NOTES

Topic:	Date: / /

ACTIONS TO TAKE

Date: / /

1
....

2
....

3
....

4
....

5
....

6
....

7
....

8
....

9
....

10
....

11
....

12
....

NOTES

Topic:	Date: / /

ACTIONS TO TAKE

Date: / /

1

2

3

4

5

6

7

8

9

10

11

12

NOTES

Topic:	Date: / /

ACTIONS TO TAKE

Date: /   /

1
....

2
....

3
....

4
....

5
....

6
....

7
....

8
....

9
....

10
....

11
....

12
....

NOTES

Topic:	Date: / /

ACTIONS TO TAKE

Date: /   /

1

2

3

4

5

6

7

8

9

10

11

12

NOTES

Topic:	Date: / /

ACTIONS TO TAKE

Date: /   /

1
....

2
....

3
....

4
....

5
....

6
....

7
....

8
....

9
....

10
....

11
....

12
....

NOTES

Date: / /

ACTIONS TO TAKE

Date: /   /

1
....

2
....

3
....

4
....

5
....

6
....

7
....

8
....

9
....

10
....

11
....

12
....

NOTES

Topic:	Date: / /

ACTIONS TO TAKE

1
....

2
....

3
....

4
....

5
....

6
....

7
....

8
....

9
....

10
....

11
....

12
....

....

NOTES

Date: / /

ACTIONS TO TAKE

Date: / /

1
....

2
....

3
....

4
....

5
....

6
....

7
....

8
....

9
....

10
....

11
....

12
....

NOTES

Topic:	Date: / /

ACTIONS TO TAKE

Date: / /

1

2

3

4

5

6

7

8

9

10

11

12

NOTES

Topic: | Date: /   /

ACTIONS TO TAKE

Date: /   /

1

2

3

4

5

6

7

8

9

10

11

12

NOTES

ACTIONS TO TAKE

Date: /   /

1
....

2
....

3
....

4
....

5
....

6
....

7
....

8
....

9
....

10
....

11
....

12
....

NOTES

Topic:	Date: / /

ACTIONS TO TAKE

Date: / /

1

2

3

4

5

6

7

8

9

10

11

12

NOTES

Topic:	Date: / /

ACTIONS TO TAKE

Date: /   /

1
....

2
....

3
....

4
....

5
....

6
....

7
....

8
....

9
....

10
....

11
....

12
....

....

NOTES

| Topic: | Date: / / |

ACTIONS TO TAKE

Date: / /

1
....

2
....

3
....

4
....

5
....

6
....

7
....

8
....

9
....

10
....

11
....

12
....

NOTES

Date: / /

ACTIONS TO TAKE

Date: /   /

1

2

3

4

5

6

7

8

9

10

11

12

NOTES

Topic: | Date: / /

ACTIONS TO TAKE

Date: /   /

1

2

3

4

5

6

7

8

9

10

11

12

NOTES

Topic:	Date: / /

ACTIONS TO TAKE

Date: / /

1
....

2
....

3
....

4
....

5
....

6
....

7
....

8
....

9
....

10
....

11
....

12
....

NOTES

Topic:	Date: / /

ACTIONS TO TAKE

1

2

3

4

5

6

7

8

9

10

11

12

NOTES

Topic: Date: /   /

ACTIONS TO TAKE

Date: /   /

1

2

3

4

5

6

7

8

9

10

11

12

NOTES

Topic:	Date: / /

ACTIONS TO TAKE

Date: /   /

1

2

3

4

5

6

7

8

9

10

11

12

NOTES

ACTIONS TO TAKE

Date: / /

1

2

3

4

5

6

7

8

9

10

11

12

NOTES

Topic:	Date: / /

ACTIONS TO TAKE

Date: / /

1

2

3

4

5

6

7

8

9

10

11

12

NOTES

Topic:	Date: / /

ACTIONS TO TAKE

Date: / /

1
....

2
....

3
....

4
....

5
....

6
....

7
....

8
....

9
....

10
....

11
....

12
....

....

NOTES

ACTIONS TO TAKE

Date: /   /

1

2

3

4

5

6

7

8

9

10

11

12

WHAT ELSE?

WHAT ELSE?

WHAT ELSE?

WHAT ELSE?

ADDITIONAL TOOLS

RACI =
Responsible, Accountable, Consulted and Informed

RACI is a responsibility matrix to identify, clarify, and define project or goal-related responsibilities. Similar models include RAPID and DACI.

Change Management

Change management models are useful for helping the organization work through elements of transition. Every leader should have at least one model they refer to often. Kotter, McKinsey, ADKAR and Lewin are just a few to consider.

Want to Have Better Conversations?

Use our proven method: A.P.S.E.A.™

A   Articulate the Challenge [issue or topic]

P   Pause and Listen

S   Show Support

E   Explore Obstacles and Options

A   Action and Accountability

APSEA™ is a trademark of Pamela J. Green Solutions, LLC

ABOUT THE AUTHOR

Pamela J. Green

Pamela J. Green is an Executive Coach and Consultant who focuses her practice on the development of executives and their teams, advancing executives, and those seeking leadership development. She is a highly sought-after consultant, executive coach, speaker and trainer with more than 30 years of leadership and executive expertise.

Lead Yourself
Lead Others
Lead Your Organization

Pamela and her team excel at equipping current and future executives, their leaders and their organizations with strategies to transform cultures that strengthen employee alignment and activate innovation and creativity. To learn more about our executive coaching and development opportunities:

Connect with Pamela on LinkedIn
www.linkedin.com/in/pamelajgreen

Follow her insights on Twitter
@pamelajgreen

Join her community of leaders at
www.pamelajgreen.com

Get a little more relaxed, and a lot more personal through Facebook:
www.facebook.com/CoachPamelaJCreen

Take our team for a test drive:
customercare@pamelajgreen.com